A Note to Parents and Teachers

Discovery Readers are nonfiction books designed for the beginning reader. Each Discovery Reader is filled with informative text, short sentences, and colorful and whimsical illustrations.

Discovery Readers make nonfiction subjects fun and historical subjects come alive. But nonfiction stories must use some words that cannot be changed for easier ones. For this reason, we encourage you to help the child with the short vocabulary list below before he or she begins the book. Learning these words will make reading the story easier.

Vocabulary List

February	New Salem
Abraham	legislature
Lincoln	United States
Indiana	Emancipation
Sarah	Proclamation
Bush	Memorial
Johnston	Washington
Kentucky	

ISBN 0-8249-5506-4

Published by Ideals Children's Books
An imprint of Ideals Publications
A division of Guideposts
535 Metroplex Drive, Suite 250
Nashville, Tennessee 37211
www.idealsbooks.com

R.L. 2.5 Spache

Library of Congress Cataloging-in-Publication Data on file

Designed by Jenny Eber Hancock

Printed in Italy by LEGO

10 9 8 7 6 5 4 3 2 1

Discover
ABRAHAM LINCOLN

STORYTELLER • LAWYER • PRESIDENT

WRITTEN BY PATRICIA A. PINGRY

ILLUSTRATED BY STEPHANIE McFETRIDGE BRITT

ideals children's books™
Nashville, Tennessee

On February 12, we
honor the birthday
of Abraham Lincoln.

Abraham was born
in 1809 in Kentucky.
His parents were poor.
They lived in a tiny log cabin.

When Abraham was eight, his
family moved north to Indiana.

Abraham helped his father
cut down trees.
He helped build a log cabin.

Life was hard in
the Indiana wilderness.

When Abraham was nine,
his mother died.

Abraham and his older sister,
Sarah, went to school.
They learned to
read and write.

When spring came, Abraham
had to leave school.
He had to help his
father on the farm.

One day, Abraham's father
brought home his new bride.

Her name was
Sarah Bush Johnston.

She told Abraham stories
about life in Kentucky.
He told her about the
books he had read.

They became good friends.
Abraham called her "Mama."
She made him feel special.

Abraham loved to read.
He borrowed books
from other people.
Sometimes he walked many
miles to get a book.

Then he walked many
miles to return it.
At night Abraham read
by the light of the fire.

Abraham grew tall and strong.
He still worked on his father's farm.
He cut down trees.
He built fences.

Then the Lincolns moved again.
They moved to Illinois.
Abraham helped his father
build another log cabin.

Then Abraham said
goodbye to his family.
He moved to a small town
named New Salem.

Abraham got a job in a store.
He liked to talk to customers.
He told them funny stories.
He even wrestled the
local champ and won!

Abraham made many friends
in New Salem.
In 1834, Abraham
ran for the state legislature.
He won that too!

Abraham wanted to be a lawyer.
He wanted to help other people.
But he was too poor to go to college.

So he read law for three years.
Abraham was a good lawyer.
People called him "Honest Abe."

One day Abraham met
a young woman from Kentucky.
Her name was Mary Todd.

Abraham thought she was beautiful.
He asked Mary to marry him.
They had four sons.

In 1860, Abraham
ran for president.
States in the South had slaves.
Abraham said that
slavery was wrong.

The South did not want
Abraham for president.
But he was elected anyway.
Abraham became the sixteenth
president of the United States.

The Lincolns moved into
the White House.
Abraham's two young sons
rode their pony on
the White House lawn.

Their goat sometimes slept in their
bed. Abraham loved having
his boys in the White House.
He laughed at their games.
They laughed at his stories.

Then the South declared
itself a separate country.
They attacked the United States.
The Civil War began.

On January 1, 1863, Abraham
signed the "Emancipation Proclamation."
Now all the slaves in
the United States were free.

After five years of war,
Lincoln's army won.

The North and South
were one country again.
There was peace.

We built the Lincoln
Memorial in Washington
to honor Abraham.

His picture is on
our five-dollar bills
and on our pennies.

Abraham was an honest lawyer.
He told funny stories.
And he was a great president.
He saved our country
and made us all free.